MONEY AND RAIN: TOM WAYMAN LIVE!

MONEY AND RAIN: TOM WAYMAN LIVE!

Macmillan of Canada / Toronto

ACKNOWLEDGEMENTS

Poems here have appeared in or been accepted for: *The Little Magazine, Poetry Northwest, Saturday Night, Sound Heritage, Copperfield, New, Quarry, Queen's Quarterly, The University of Windsor Review, The Capilano Review, The Ontario Review, The Lamp in the Spine, The Minnesota Review, The Fiddlehead, The Canadian Forum, This Magazine, kayak, Criteria, The Malahat Review.*

"The Return" was first published in Walter Lowenfels, ed., *For Neruda, For Chile,* Beacon Press, Boston, 1975. I am also grateful for a bursary from the Canada Council in 1972-73, which gave time for some of these poems.

This book is in memory of Patrick McNulty; and it is

for my brother Mike.

ISBN 0-7705-1310-7

Printed in Canada for
The Macmillan Company of Canada Limited
70 Bond Street, Toronto M5B 1X3

CONTENTS

THE CHILEAN ELEGIES

THE KISS AND THE CRY

If you can see the mountains, it is going to rain.
If you can't, it's raining.

—B.C. Coast folk saying

FRIENDS

"I want to start with a poem about Vancouver, where I live. In the long evenings here, sometimes the air before dark turns a certain shade of blue in color. When this happens, after a while it seems as though every object in the City takes on the same shade, the same blue.

"This poem is about that, called The Blue Hour . . .*"*

THE BLUE HOUR

The blue hour begins
on the North Shore mountains
flows down to the harbor's edge
and into the blue blanket of City.
This evening the air has turned
a deep marine blue, that settles over the roads and houses
street lamps and neon, muting the detail of
telephone poles, trees, and the angle of roofs
so the low hills of blue become the ground swell
to a blue anthem, points of light everywhere across it
the ten thousand notes of a song: chorus of downtown
and West End, then the long verses of Kitsilano,
Marpole, Mount Pleasant, Grandview
and the far reach to Capitol Hill.

The color calms the blue water
stretching west past the flashes of Point Atkinson's light
and threads in again among
the tugs and sawdust barges
headed slowly up the Fraser's still north arm.

In this hour, a bus
which has blazed the name of my City
across half a continent
rolls in at last with its riding lights burning
moving up the Oak Street Bridge through the blue air.

"But it is what is happening to the people of my City that preoccupies me: what is happening to myself, and my friends, as we move through our time alive here, through the only part of history in which we can live . . "

RAINSHADOW

Rain in the afternoon: the City in a grey light.
The downpour touches the window, sounds on the adjoining roofs
and drips over the eaves, falling onto the stairs of wooden porches
down to the ground. City of rain:
low hills under rain at the gate of the mountains.

City with the Dutch name of an English sea-captain
in the rain, at the Pacific's edge.

In an old hut in the rain, in this City
I sat in a room and began.
I looked for a long time at a photograph from a magazine
of boys armed with automatic rifles
standing in another forest far away.
It did not seem to me they were much, not so much
as had been said about them. Then, later on
they were everything. And today, not so much again.

This afternoon I am moving in my twenty-eighth year
of rain, through the wreck and fringes of a motion
that had no centre—unless it was
in the midst of a jostling crowd chanting phrases, or with
the lone and certain young man
carefully packing his fear and dynamite around the leg
of a statue. But neither of these was central to me.
I began with uneasiness: something that went wrong with a life
and the lives around me, injustice

and from this a new idea, that explained so well
how every part linked and meshed with each other
that I understood if you sold someone a leaflet
already you had eased a black man's pain in Angola.

For more than poets, we believed in the power of words.
All anyone had to do was read, to agree
and to agree, to join. Nothing else was possible
and it was already happening.
We accepted the old lie that the truth would make people free.
So we sold them the truth, or gave it away
and waited for their indifference to turn into a regiment.

There was also an understanding that the life of the self
could only be realized by denying it, selflessly
taking orders, obediently following a leadership.
Worse, there was an understanding that we were the leadership:
that the only way forward was our way, that what we wanted
was what everyone wanted, if they only understood themselves
as well as we understood them, and gave up wanting
what it was they thought they wanted, or in any case
they would learn to want what we wanted in time.

And then I learned that when you try to start again,
to plot your way through this madness, there is a face
that rises and agrees. You decide that you share
enemies in common, that this unites you, but then you feel

you should demur about such-and-such, that he isn't really a threat
and about X, that he isn't dangerous, and should be denounced
or about Y, that he doesn't need watching. While you argue
about these excesses, suddenly you find yourself denying
that you, too, are in league with the foe. Now all of your energy
goes to explain everything you have recently said, to prove this.
Those whom you wished to convince of the general state of things
meantime look on. You are a little ashamed
flustered that all this infighting will turn them away.
You need not have worried. They understand failure.
They were taught it early in school, like you, and rehearsed it
most of their lives. They do not reject you for what you have said
but because they now know you for one of themselves
—hopeless, for all your fantasy and prayer.

And the rain falls into the street
with its rows of jobs, indifferent and boring, the tedious hours
logged for money, or the work that has to be lifted
gasping for air, at the edge of what the body can do
so there is nothing thought of in the body but black rage
or sleep, in the job that goes on like the rain, like the lives
not rich but correct and borrowed
filled with somebody else's images, skin and clothes and apartment rooms
interchangeable, replaceable, where the only sign of the occupant
all they have put their mark on
is the particular shape of the rolled-up toothpaste tube

on the smooth bathroom sink, and the specific amounts of hair,
bobby pins and old kleenex they have in their waste tins.

Yet these lives too, when you know them
possess an uneasiness, a sense of something beyond the perpetual music
that is wrong with a life, a deep silence
in the midst of a party that is not supposed to be there:
an impatience with the rain.

Mostly I love my City in the rain, when it is as a forest
on a dark evening, the drops blown down
and falling from the trees and buildings and the grey sky:
no sound but the water falling and a wind—
night rain on the window, the wet lights—
spring rain on the new leaves and the City and the water falling
twenty-eight years and no end.

"One of the ways I have amused myself during the past half-dozen years in Vancouver is by applying for jobs in the English departments of various colleges and universities. I taught for a year in a university in Colorado just after I graduated, but somehow since then nobody has seen that I am obviously the best man for whatever position is being offered.

"One day I noted down all the reasons I had been given for being turned down for these teaching jobs, and came up with a poem called Not Getting Hired . . ."

NOT GETTING HIRED

"Writing? This is an *English* department.
Frankly I can't see what use a writer could be."
And also: "Only one book? My friend,
we have literally dozens of applications from poets.
Unless you've done more than this, I'm afraid you'll just go in the pile."

As well, there was a Bursar and Dean of Instruction
who became incensed at Wayman's subversive notions:
"That's how you'd mark an English paper? Do you never use
any other criteria besides your own subjective opinions?
Just answer the question, Mr. Wayman: yes or no."
There was one of a selection committee who invited Wayman
to attend a lecture on Marxist Aesthetics that afternoon.
In the silence that followed Wayman's reply, the Head
leaned forward gravely: "All of us in the Department are going
you know. We'd be very interested
in your reasons for not wishing to attend."

Then there was an appointment for nine p.m., after a long day
dragging boards all around a jobsite. "Enthusiasm, man!"
the Dean of Curriculum and Instruction wanted, as he pounded
one arm of his chair. "Think big. This college is going places.
You'll have to step lively if you want to come along with us."
And there was a university Wayman was keen to impress, where he spoke
with great speed and skill about his plans, his hopes, his ideas.
Later, Wayman heard the Chairman had thoughtfully fingered

a small white pamphlet after Wayman left.
"And did you notice his pupils?" the Chairman had asked.
"How large they were? Obviously, the man is on drugs."

Everywhere, the impossible gigantic question:
"Now if you were setting up a basic composition program
how would you go about it?" And: "We find in our classes sometimes
we can utilize other media besides print. How do you feel about this?"
One night, a horrible dream
in which Wayman goes to see Neil at the site
to ask for his old job back, and finds Neil has appointed
a selection committee: Danny, Pat Flynn and John Davies
sit waiting amid the scaffolds and sawdust.
Danny asks the first question: "Now, Wayman,
lately we've been putting our gyproc nails
eight inches apart. What are your thoughts on that?"

Everyone's eyes turn toward him, watching.

"As well as not getting hired, one of the interesting things that has happened to me over the years is that I have managed to publish a couple of books of poems. But I have discovered that instead of that making me into a poet, it has made me into a crank.

"You know what a crank is: a person who can babble for hours about his strange ideas on a topic. When my first book Waiting For Wayman *was published, I found myself to my surprise becoming one of these cranks . . ."*

BECOMING A CRANK

In the clutches of his publishers, Wayman became a crank.
It had to do with Wayman's continually expressed opinions
on who buys poetry and why. It had to do with the publishers
carefully ignoring his obviously lucrative ideas.
There *was* a letter from the Director of Advertising, Promotion, and Publicity
welcoming Wayman as "a great addition to the Spring List"
but that had Wayman's first name wrong.
And at the end, there were disagreements about price,
the size, the format, typeface, interior spacing, cover artwork
and a few miscellaneous corrections
—all of which Wayman lost. Unable to generate any responsive spark
Wayman became the crank.

He knew he was a crank when, at a local sales party
he found he could start in about his complaints
while keeping all his attention on the drinks and food.
He knew he was a crank when, as he began to explain his views
to the firm's regional representative
the latter said: "Oh, here is a bookseller.
He's the person you really should speak to . . ." and vanished.
Wayman was launched into it again
when suddenly the bookseller leaned forward
—a freak no older than Wayman, but with his own store—
and said: "Man, this is interesting. But, wow, am I stoned."

Wayman knew he was beat. Numbly getting his hat and coat

he met the Publisher himself, fresh off his plane from the East.
"I just want to let you know we'll do everything we can for you,"
the Publisher said grandly. "Thank you very much," Wayman said
without a trace of irony in his voice,
"I appreciate that." And walking away with his book
—his poor, hard-bound, high-priced, undersold book—
Wayman heard from behind his Publisher say:
"Please don't mention it. After all, it's our *job*."

"With a little urging, I could probably become a crank on the subject of ecology, too. This next poem, which is sort of about ecology, was suggested by a line uttered by my friend Pat Flynn.

"The line is in the poem, but I won't say which one it is. That way, if you like it as much as I do, you might think that I wrote it. Instead, I'd like to dedicate the entire poem to him . . ."

EARTH SHOT

for Pat Flynn

All of the plants watched the moon shot.
Those that were captured, and forced to live in tiny pots
inside men's houses, saw it directly on television.
But deep in the forest, the majority viewed it internally
picking up the electrons through their radiation-sensitive skins.

The green world could hear the animals cheer
as these clustered around the few TV sets in the woods.
An old Bear summed it up for the chipmunks and foxes,
the racoons and deermice all watching ecstatic with joy.
"It's a small step for a man," Bear said amid applause,
"but it's a giant leap for the animal kingdom."

The firs said nothing. Not a sound from the tiniest moss
or the ferns. They might have shown how the deed was impossible
without their continued participation with regard to the air.
Or pointed out how the grasses alone outnumber the animals
if anyone wants to start considering "planetary co-operation
and achievement". But they didn't.

There's a small step the green world is working on
and all of them know it. It's a small step
for each of them, but it's a giant leap for the plants

and the whales.

"Being a little weird in my opinions on a few subjects, I find I am attracted to stories about people who have interesting quirks themselves. There used to be a hardware store next to the place where I bank which was owned by a woman who, as nearly as anyone could figure out, ran the entire business as a hobby . . ."

WHAT THE BANK SEES

The woman who owned the bank building
also owned the adjoining hardware store.
She tended the store herself, whenever she felt like it.
The girls in the bank said lots of times
they'd be sent out for supplies—rolls of scotch tape or
boxes of paper clips—and always the store would be closed.
There were few deposits to the store's account:
when she did make them, mostly it was her pension cheque,
the bank's rent, or cash from the tenants of her houses.

An entire hardware store, the stock aging and dusty.
Imagine going in there and asking for something she didn't have.
Would she say she would order it for you
and when you went back you found the place closed as usual?
Maybe she took orders for things on an old scratch pad
and crumpled up the request and threw it away
after the customer left? The bank wanted her to sell out
so they could expand, but she wouldn't.

Then one afternoon her younger sister
asked to be let into the vault
to get the will out of their safety deposit box.
That day, too, the hardware store
stayed closed, in her honor.

"Elderly men and women are traditionally cranks, people with quirks. I have a poem here about an encounter with one of these that happened to me when I was walking through Vancouver's West End just after the first cease-fire in Viet Nam was announced.

"I liked this old man a lot since his prejudices pretty well match mine. Actually, people have told me I'm going to make a good little-old-man myself. Anyway, this poem is called Canada At War . . ."

CANADA AT WAR

"I'm glad the war's over . . ." a cheerful voice
". . . so no more young men like yourself will be blown to bits."

A faded blue suit and cane had stopped on the sidewalk
and was smiling at me with old, thin teeth.

"Shell got me, high explosive, blew my right foot off,"
the voice said pleasantly. "But the shell
had a tumble on it so it rounded the end of the bone."
A block away, the trees and benches of English Bay's promenade;
the blue ocean lying beyond in the early Spring sun.

"Those officers," the man said. "This one wanted us
to go up a hill to get some bricks for his safety-first dugout.
Our sergeant, he refused. It was already light, you see
and the Germans could shoot at us there from three sides.

"But there were lots of officers like that. They were all over
England, strutting around." The man suddenly straightened, grinning,
put a swagger stick under one armpit and marched
important for an instant in the Army of another time.

"The bastards would come out as far as our third-line support trenches.
Then they could go back and wear a ribbon, here, 'returned soldier'
because they had been to France.

"This officer pulled his revolver out
and points it right at our sergeant. *Sergeant*, he says,

are you going to obey my order? So the sergeant
gets us together and says *I want you to go out single file*
six yards apart. That way if a shell lands
you won't all be killed. We made it to the farmhouse;
plenty of bricks there. Because I was the shortest
I was supposed to hold the bags open while the others shovelled.
Then the shell lands, and blows me over and over. The rest
made it into a little dugout about the distance to that car.
Bobby Johnston sticks his head out
and yells *Jess, Jess are you all right?*
They thought I was done for. *I'm okay Bobby*
I yell back, *but you keep down.* Then another shell lands
and two pieces of shrapnel catch him in the neck.
So there's the two of us lying out there. And my leg is
starting to hurt, like a toothache, but all over and much worse.
Shells are landing regularly, and I don't mind saying
I was shaking so badly I was vibrating like this
against the ground. They got out to me at last with a stretcher
but they had to drag it back to the dugout
crawling along the ground. The Germans could shoot at that hill
you see, from three sides. And they shelled us there
from seven to eleven-thirty, when I guess they had to stop
to cool their guns.

"Oh," he says, "I could tell you stories.
At the time, you know, they said we were fighting for Jesus Christ.

What a laugh. With the Pope and the Church of England
putting their money into armaments while we fought.
But I'm glad I lost the foot. I got my pension for it.
Otherwise, when I came back, I'd likely have been unemployed.
Before the war I'd been a sailor for a while on the Great Lakes
and done a little logging, and on the farm.
Afterwards, I was lucky to have that pension.

"Well, I could talk to you all day," he said
and turned, and began moving down the street again toward the water.

"Encounters like the one in the last poem are a way that history comes alive for me, through hearing the words and feelings of those who lived through earlier times. One continuing concern of mine is the use we make of history: what is it we choose to remember and what lessons if any we draw from the past.

"In 1973 when I was on vacation on Vancouver Island I went to a National Historic Park near Victoria, where with elaborate detail and fine museum techniques the whole history of coast defense in the Victoria area is preserved.

"I certainly enjoyed the display, but I kept asking myself, is this what we want to preserve of our past? Especially because this whole display is a monument to nothing happening . . . the guns were never fired. Whereas there is an incredible history of work and bloodshed and struggle on Vancouver Island of which virtually nothing has been preserved, and certainly not with the painstaking care and accuracy of a National Historic Park . . ."

FORT RODD HILL NATIONAL HISTORIC PARK

Sunshine on the wide June water
under a faultless sky. Below Fort Rodd Hill
the Strait of Juan de Fuca runs out to a blank horizon
as though to the Pacific itself. This is what the watchers saw
for sixty years.

The lip of the trench of Upper Battery:
the eyes of Fort Rodd stood here, protected by steel
in the Night Fire Command Post, or by the glass
of the range finders.

Coast defense: in 1854 the Royal Navy
arrived off Victoria with sick and wounded
from the war in Russia. Nothing here could aid them
so the fleet sailed south to the naval base at Valparaiso
Chile. Then the British began to build Esquimalt.
In 1878 the new Dominion
borrowed English guns to protect the area
during the Russo-Turkish war. Fifteen years later
all this was obsolete, so Canada and the Imperial Government
agreed jointly to arm batteries at
Signal Hill, Fort Rodd Hill, Macaulay Point, Belmont, Duntze Head
and Black Rock. Fort Rodd had
three six-inch guns for ranges up to 10,000 yards
with Belmont, along the point, mounting two twelve-pounder
quick-firing guns plus searchlights.
All this by 1896. Around the Fort Rodd installations

a loop-holed concrete wall protects the gunners
from enemy shore parties: the loop-holes are
funnel-shaped through the wall, the broadest portion inside
for the widest possible fields of fire.
Where cliffs at the edge of Upper and Lower Battery
make ground assault unlikely
the high grey walls stop and a tangle of staked barbed wire
shields the position. Inside the sunken batteries
—each with water storage, crew shelters, magazine—
the gunners drilled and waited.

At first these were Englishmen, Royal Garrison Artillery
paid for from Dominion funds. Later on they learned
this was as Canadian as anyone gets, and by 1906
the gunners were officially Canadian. In 1938
the defenses were modernized for the next war
and by 1956 the system was obsolete again and became Historic.

Sixty years of Canadians waiting to enter history.
Sixty years of paranoia or preparedness
—whatever the term—that we call history because
it has to do with someone else's history.
Strange to think that on this distant coast
they would erect so clumsy a part of Europe
and Europe's wars, and that we would honor and preserve it.

Behind these guns, north through the bush

the Island coalminers lived another kind of history: everyday
food prices, getting hired, days off and
days on, the work that made the Island worth protecting.
These entered history too, not out of their daily tasks
but only when they stood together against death:
coal gas in the pits, digging at the coalface knee deep in water,
buying and storing their own powder
and the robbery of crooked weigh scales, company stores
and company housing. They enter history in the great strikes
when the Army moved against them. They took the only shots
fired in anger at white men in this Island.

Now the mines lie under the rainforest. The slagmounds left
at Extension shadow the houses that remain in the tiny valley.
The shafts have disappeared under dynamite and alder in the hills.
The Jinglepot mine behind Nanaimo
had a pitch so steep that the miners could only walk down
with difficulty, a seventy-degree slope, and at shift change
the men were hauled up behind railcars
that lifted the firebosses: each car trailed a long rope
which the men grasped and so were pulled out of the pit.
Now the Jinglepot and its townsite
are a few square feet in a wood: some half-buried timbers
and old rails bent into the wet ground and overgrown.

Unlike the house of Fort Rodd's Master Gunner
the house of an Island coalminer

will not be preserved: his alarm clock, calendar, washpail, bed,
his clothes, what he had to eat and what he looked like.
No one will detail what he did in his life
or who were his family. Less than a hundred years of work
burned out these men and women so that they vanished
like coal, like coast defense. Nothing is their monument.
Now they are gone they do not mean a single thing:

like you, like me.

"At one point I became fascinated by the life of one of the early Vancouver Island coalminers, a man called Ginger Goodwin.

"Goodwin was an Englishman who came to B.C. at some point to work in the coalmines at Cumberland, about 10 miles inland from Courtenay, when a lot of mining was going on there before the First World War.

"He got involved with the union movement, the strikes, and was another of those people who didn't believe the First World War was really the war to end war and all that. He was called up for conscription, but like a number of others evaded the draft by hiding out in the Cumberland area. However, he was discovered and killed in the bush by a policeman. The day Goodwin was buried, August 2, 1918, the first general strike in B.C. was held in Vancouver to protest his death . . ."

CUMBERLAND GRAVEYARD, FEBRUARY 1973

I stand with one hand on the wet uneven rock
that marks the grave of Ginger Goodwin
at Cumberland cemetery in the drizzle of
a Wednesday afternoon: a meadow hacked out of the rainforest
littered with old and new stone markers,
grey cement slabs, and the damp mounds of fresh earth.

In the rain, Cumberland graveyard
looks like the one on Kaien Island where I grew up
in the shadow of Mount Hays, where people said
*I'd hate to be buried there and have rainwater
trickling down my back forever.*

But they got buried anyway. And here
there are not so many graves as I thought
considering the long chain of coalmine disasters
that ran south from here seventy miles, for nearly
one hundred years. There are few markers that say
Killed in an Explosion in No. 4 Mine; Aged 17 years.
When people get around to putting up stones
they don't seem to care how death arrives, but carve:
Only Sleeping; Lo, I am with you always; and *Gone Home.*
Lots of the graves are neglected now—not as abandoned
as the Chinese cemetery half a mile up the road—
but inscriptions have worn away, headstones tilted
and cracked, and here a slab of old pebbly concrete

above some graves shakes as you walk on it. A few of these slabs
have sagged and split open. You can crouch
and peer in, but inside is only the top of more wet earth
and a few broken plastic flowers
blown across and down from the more modern graves.

A strange familiarity appears in the plots marked
Gran, or *Papa, Mama* and *Mary,* or
In loving memory of our son Tommy, when now
no one can make out the surname. And where the graves
are clear as the Hudson family's, say
—infants, children, parents and the last date in the 1950s—
what would bring anyone out in this rain
to stand looking at the letters chiselled into the blocks of soaking stone?

But Goodwin's grave differs from these.
Not that it's by itself, on the contrary
you could just about get another one beside him
but the rest of the way around he's completely hemmed in
and there's a new pile of wet earth not 10 feet away.
Yet Goodwin seems buried
for another reason than these: nobody bothered to put
his birthdate on his stone, for example,
just that he was *Shot, July 26th, 1918.*
And the lettering isn't nearly as regular
as on the other stones: *Lest We Forget* it says
and it's about as professional as a title

someone has put on a pamphlet they've printed
overnight, trying their best with the letters
but not doing so well, and the whole thing soon forgotten
anyway. On the top of the stone
is a crude sickle and hammer—done
as though in the years before there were Commies,
when those who thought a certain way were sure
that what had just happened in Russia
had something in it for them. Like the words
it's an amateur's job: the sort of sickle and hammer
someone might carve if he'd only heard about it
or seen it drawn by hand on a piece of paper. Under it all
in place of a slogan, it says *A Worker's Friend*
like a dog is man's best friend, except that the worn cement curb
that outlines the grave is exactly the size
of a man, not so small as a child or as large as a family.

The afternoon I was there, the grooves in the rock
that form the words were painted black, with fresh red color
for the verb "shot" and the symbol above.
And that's the secret to this wet grave, this poem
and the dripping old coal town: somebody there
drops by once in a while to see how this rock
bears up under the weather. Maybe only one old man
an ex-miner who lives on in this valley
where the trees have covered the slag heaps and hills

but are going themselves higher up, missing
in vast swathes cut across the mountains. One old man
in the rain and maybe nobody knows exactly who
and won't until he dies also and then two graves
will decay together, or maybe only one
because who puts up stones for old miners now
when the last mine closed twenty years ago
and no one can say when the old man last worked anyhow?

But right now that oldtimer
is keeping a dream going.
Strange to think of a town like Cumberland
having a dream, after all the lives squeezed from it
—in just a second underground
or in unendurable years and days and hours
aboveground and down, all the grinding horror
of living a Company life for a Company lifetime.
But we know it was Cumberland's dream
at least for a day, because everyone says at that time
a mile of the town appeared to bury Goodwin:
a mile of miners and women and kids
which is a lot of people to bury anybody
especially if they aren't being paid to do it.

Strange to think of a town like Cumberland
not only having a dream, but a hero:
an honest-to-something hero (I don't see

how I can call him less
since he came out of nowhere particular
that anyone knows, and worked in the mines
and struck in the strikes of '13
when the great Canadian militia
terrorized the coalfields for a year, before going off
to die like pigs in the muddy barnyard of France.
And Goodwin meanwhile
didn't kill anybody,
kept working away for a better life
up at Trail, became secretary of the miners there
fighting conscription while he could
and when Blaylock and Cominco wanted him dead
or out of there at least, he went—
though on his own terms—hiding out here
until he was shot in the back for it.)

And Goodwin didn't kill anyone
to be a hero, not even a scab or a German
or an Indian, as far as we know, but he thought
and read and he wrote, and he talked to people
—we know all that—and he went to lots of meetings
and probably called too many of them himself.
But because he could do all these things, he was a little different
than the man beside him, but he was anyway, really
—that being the way things are—though this difference

plus having a sort of dream
landed him flat on his back under this rainy meadow
a little earlier than his consumption likely would have gotten him here.

And that's all. I walk out of the graveyard gate
as he can't do any more, and cross the wet asphalt
to the car. He's behind us now, like being wakened in the night
and having the dream you were in hesitate in your mind for a second
then slip down through a hole in the net of the night
and vanish into the solid dark wall of black air.
That dream is lost, what it was forgotten
unless, even years later,
you start another dream in which suddenly you are aware
this is a dream you began once before.

38

"Part of my fascination with the history of everyday life extends toward our physical setting, the objects that surround us. Here is a poem that tries to enter into the life of a room in an apartment building, a room we live in for only a while and then leave. The poem is trying to look at the room from the point of view of the floor . . ."

WHAT THE FLOOR SEES

At first the window frames look down indifferently.
They have seen so much furniture arrive and go.
Below them the chairs huddle to the table
staying close to what is familiar here.
The old sofa sits stiffly, like a portly, retired officer
living with as much dignity as he can in a rented room.
He has lived in so many rooms, among so many different people
that he relies only on himself now for his feeling of importance.

But after a week, the window relents.
It stops being aloof, starts to accept the new furniture.
A month later they are great friends.
Then at last, when the furniture is piled by the door
to be moved out again, the window frames are saddened, numb.
Whatever comes into the place next will find them
empty, withdrawn, musing about other things.

40

"It seems to me that what surrounds us, besides the places and objects of our daily life, is our friends. This is a poem about how we sometimes feel our friends aren't exactly what we might have wanted for ourselves . . . which is also how we feel about where we live and what we do.

"Still, they are what we live among, where we are . . ."

FRIENDS

All of them accidents, like getting born
or being at a party: who happens to arrive at it,
a good conversation in the hallway, dancing real close
in the darkened front room, never what you actually planned
would occur, nor what you would want.
But a knock on the door and they crowd in
perch all over the bed and chairs, spill their beer
on the rug, melt a record by leaving it on top of the amplifier
by mistake, and eat everything in the fridge.

Maybe this is all there is. Jobs come and go like new women:
when you don't have them you want them
but when you get them you'd rather be elsewhere
driving around alone. But friends
go on like a sort of family that stays in touch
through arguments and silences and going out to a movie together
until one day it's brought up short, reshuffled
baffled by death or a divorce or somebody moving away.

Maybe this is all there is, more than the little presents
of mail every day or brand new celery or
just-wrapped hamburger: miniature Christmases and
daily birthdays that are almost routine. Your horrible friends
fill up the time between getting born and dying
give as much pleasure as poems and in fact

last longer than poems.

I remember the words' flash, the turn of their wit in the air
faced with a vision of what is: boredom now and nothing later
but the fall of gritty rain into an oil-slick sea,
a thin soapy surf of foam on the beach
at the edge of these logged-off mountains.
Words aren't much to stack against living: talk,
going out for a beer, a number of complicated moments
on the job or in bed, or just walking around.

And my friends at last are all that remains of me.
More than any words, these are what gets left of my living body
my cantankerous, itchy, glandular columns of meat:
how it moved in the air among them
got itself dressed up and also undressed
let loose some magnificent farts, failed and fell down
at work sometimes, was frightened crossing a high log
on a trail, or refused to watch horror movies
was always uptight and babbled on at them
calling them its unfortunate friends.

"*Now, one thing almost all my friends do, whether they are lawyers or laborers,
is smoke up lots of the dreaded killer weed, marijuana. With so much puffing and
coughing going on, one would think there would be many poems about smoking the
stuff. When tobacco, for example, first began to be popular in Elizabethan England,
people wrote poems about that. Here is one by Tobias Hume, published in 1605:*

> Tobacco, Tobacco,
> Sing sweetly for Tobacco,
> Tobacco is like love,
> O love it,
> For you see I will prove it.
>
> Love makes leane the fatte mens tumor,
>   So doth Tobacco,
> Love still dries uppe the wanton humor,
>   So doth Tobacco,
> Love makes men sayle from shore to shore,
>   So doth Tobacco,
> Tis fond love often makes men poor,
>   So doth Tobacco,
> Love makes men scorne al Coward feares,
>   So doth Tobacco,
> Love often sets men by the eares,
>   So doth Tobacco.
>
> Tobacco, Tobacco,
> Sing sweetly for Tobacco,
> Tobacco is like love,

44

O love it,
For you see I have provde it.

"My next poem is an attempt to do something like this, although unfortunately without the comic wit. The poem is called The Fire and the Rain . . .*"*

THE FIRE AND THE RAIN

The two tiny pillows of her lips
on mine, and in her breath
the hot sun of *Aztlan,*
of *California, Baja, Sonora*
shrivels her, her rich mouth turned to paper
my lady *marijuana*

has travelled two thousand miles
from the deserts of soil and red rock,
of mesquite, and the coastal palms:
her self purchased and sold again
in a hundred grimy rooms, unspeakable things
done to her body, she arrives at the edge of this northern sea
one grey day in the rain, still full

of the sun, fierce and heavy in the brown hills
I remember, cottages on the green slope facing the ocean
picking their way down amid the roofs and palms and roadways
to beaches and coves. A porch vine
rests in the hot stillness; white walls
shadow iceplant and a violet flame of flower.

Inside
a bowl holds
coast orange, lemon,
avocado. The sounds of faint traffic,
children fade.
Bared feet feel

sand grains on the cool wood floors.

These are the long moments
a wind blows through . . .

Somehow she appears, my lady *marijuana*
drifts north like smoke carried a long way:
smoke from a fire of hunger, that withers
an entire family of *campesinos,* who vanish;
desperation that burns in another man
to whom she is merely a quick way out of the street, she fails him

and is here with me on a rainy evening
where the heat is only the electric City
merged into one wide lantern beamed at the darkness:
the dripping forest, the shoreline, and the empty sea.
In dreams she comes to me full and round and loving,
unclothed, eager to have me possess her, be inside
to give her the same joy, the ecstasy she promises.
But in person with her, all I can do is kiss
briefly, a few pecks
before her body returns to the blue light, across the room.

She does not bring me quiet.
The urge to have her fills me, I want
more of her than this, want my flesh on hers, another kind of heat
blazing in us, making us sweat together, naked here
out of the rain.

"Another thing that my friends like to do is to gossip. I have retained good friends from many of the places I have lived in, but the best source of never-ending gossip I have discovered is the people I met when teaching in a town in northern Colorado.

"I only lived there for one year, but the friends I made have stayed in close touch with me since . . . a number of them now also live in B.C. People from this town, and stories about it, seem to crop up endlessly. Sometimes it looks to me—and I know others from there feel the same way—as though this one town is the centre of an enormous web of human lives and actions, perhaps touching every person now alive. It is very strange . . ."

GOSSIP

A fire is burning in the pure air:
bright as a white illuminated plastic sign
flashing the name of a store into the night.

Fort Collins, Colorado, is the centre of the human universe.
There is a house in Fort Collins that eats itself alive.
Sometimes it lives in an oxygen tent, but sometimes
it tears this out of its mouth and stuffs booze down its throat, sobbing.
The house is eating its children.

Fort Collins is the centre of the human universe.
There are parents who have not *seen* their children
for five or six years. They try not to think about them.
When they go out with another couple after work to a cocktail lounge
each of the women imagines for an instant
the young waitress resembles her daughter .

Her daughter is in a cabin in the foothills.
She and some professors, some professors' wives
and some students are trying each other out and on.
The President of the University is a Director of the local bank.
Only he knows the direction the University is going to expand.
The young people in the hills want to buy another dozen acres
but if two of them sign a paper together it is certain they will split up.

Cameron David Bishop has made the list again
of the seven most wanted men in Canada.

This is because four years after he left Fort Collins, Colorado
Cam is still on the FBI's 10-most-wanted slate.
Appearing with him on the Canadian list is the man sought
for killing the daughter of a Vancouver English Department chairman
and her boyfriend, as the two were sleeping in the bush near Tofino.
Cam, they say, shut off the power for an afternoon to a war plant near Denver
by applying some dynamite to certain isolated power poles.

No one was hurt, but Cam had to run.
Despite this Kodak has located a new factory near Fort Collins.
Water-pik, Woodward Governor and Monfort Beef
are some other local industries. Larry Davidson
got arrested for two joints. Larry Lechner passed the union's exam
and has been working as a carpenter. Fort Collins

is the centre of the human universe.

"One advantage of having friends in many places is that you can jump in your car and go visit them. This is a poem about driving across North America, in this case up the Yellowhead Highway toward Edmonton. The poem is called Moving . . ."

MOVING

i A great wheel drives this car; a cycle:
   the fire in the cylinders flaring again and again
   as the disc of the timer swings past its contacts, the car
   speeding north from Kamloops one late afternoon
   into the forest, shafts spinning in their beds of grease
   and air, turning at last the rubber wheels
   over and down along the winding asphalt, headed
   into the early spring of the year

   past Rayleigh, Barriere, Little Fort,
   the small farms and ranches wedged in
   between the mountains, the wide river
   and the road. They scatter a debris of old tractors
   across their fields, broken wagons, collapsed buildings
   and around each occupied dwelling discarded radiators,
   wrecked cars, snowmobiles, lumber and refrigerators
   spread like a mat. I drive on

   where the first fires go up in the meadows:
   burnt stubble flickers; the refuse
   of a cleared woods, raked and bulldozed into piles
   and set alight. The fire here
   has burned the grass a dozen yards along the highway
   leaving the blackened stump of a fencepost
   crisp smoke rising gently from it, tonight

   in this month of high beef prices

the small herds have multiplied, set out to graze
in the stones and weeds of fields hardly more green
than old rocky river bottoms. I drive on

alive on the road again, out of the city,
overland in a machine just a few can repair, and so
into a sort of gamble:
speeding helplessly on into another time.

ii The rhythm, steel on steel, propels me:
everywhere becoming music.
Breakfast at Clearwater, in the café
across from the region's high school.
At eight, the young girls come in
to buy their chocolates and gum for the day,
filling the tables with boyfriends and coffee
a harassment to the glum waitress only twice their age.
In one corner the machine,
manifestation of the fluids that fuel us
with their own pumps and rhythms, clicks on
and out over the North Thompson School District
the *Rolling Stones* begin.

                    In Eugene, Oregon, once
I sat with a group of drivers listening
to a different song on the same machine, and all agreed

with the child that was me years before in Cow Bay
in a restaurant, a thousand miles northwest from here,
that the song was ours. Today, 68 miles on the highway
to Blue River, then north through the bush 56 miles to Valemount:
on without pause in the drive of the engine, the music
alive and turning on the great wheel.

54

"In 1972 I drove through the mid-western United States visiting friends I had originally gotten to know in other parts of the U.S. I wrote a couple of poems about this; the first is called Midwest Rain . . ."

MIDWEST RAIN

The rain falls into Michigan.
On an ordinary Tuesday afternoon in the autumn
I sit reading in a house built of stone.

Jones' house: rain splashes through the full leaves.
Water runs down the stone.

But an entire floor of this place was constructed under the ground.
The bathroom, kitchen and dining corner
loom in the dull green light of windows opening at the tops of the walls.
A root cellar down here, already damp with rain
holds shelves of preserves, barrels
and tubs of the first white shoots of fall-budding
poems.

The same rain later arrives in Minnesota.
I sit in my foreign car on a green-shaded street
lined with St. Paul's mansions, watching out through the downpour.
Everywhere I have driven this year I have found old friends again.
Every city or town I have stopped in I have been made welcome.

"And the second poem . . ."

AND SO I WAS SHOWN

And so I was shown
the garden of the Mississippi
where it rises to the north, in the city of lakes
in the city of falling water.
Here the river carries its first tugs and barges
into the first locks, past sandy wooded shores.
There I entered another city, a city Not Made By Hand.

Twilight on the freeways, speeding across
gold-tinted bridges: Leukemia City
beautiful here in the sunset, in that gleam and motion
a still life of the Seine winding somewhere through Paris . . .

But not Paris: St. Paul's cathedral
on the approach to the river ridge.
The settlers' trees grown huge now
shading the stone mansions of Summit Drive:

root, leaf and limb.
Red aircraft warning lamps
pulsing on far-away towers.

But best, her hair's shadow on her face
glowing in the room's dim, steady light: webs of soft lines
like shadows of tree branches seen on a tent wall.

Finding her then, in this city
in the city of lakes, breasts electrical, trembling

hot sheath of love and of oranges.
City of falling water.
Garden of the Mississippi.

THE FACTORY HOUR

for Andy,
Gus,
and John Hoskins

"In the summer of 1973 I found myself in a familiar set of circumstances: broke,
and therefore having to go out and look for a job. As I lolled on Kitsilano Beach,
thinking of my impending return to what is known as 'the industrial work force', it
came to me once again what an awful thing it is to have to tuck down and go back to
work. This is a poem about that . . ."

KITSILANO BEACH PARK: JULY 1973

High summer. A warm wind down the inlet
moves into the City from the western ocean.
Out on the sun-glinting water, a chop
drives between the sailboats; the waves
splash in at last among swimmers and their rocks and sand.

Here in the sunshine I am lying
on a grassy knoll that rises over the distant cries
and water sounds of the beach. On the inlet's other shore
the mighty wall of the West End's apartments
lifts through the sea air.

These high windy July hours
seem to me like an orchard, with every moment
a beautiful fruit—apricot, plum—
ripening somewhere on a tree.
O beautiful City, who will be here to praise your afternoons
when I have gone into your horrible factories
making each minute into a thing of metal
dusty, still coated with the grit of files and drills
able to be weighed, measured with a gauge, and sold.

"Being unable to find a job while lying on Kits Beach, though I did try, I began that process known to the Unemployment Insurance Commission as 'actively seeking employment' . . ."

Everybody was very nice. Each place Wayman went
the receptionist said: "Certainly we are hiring.
Just fill out one of these forms." Then, silence.
Wayman would call back each plant and corporation
and his telephone would explain: "Well, you see,
we do our hiring pretty much at random. Our interviewers
draw someone out of the stack of applications we have on file.
There's no telling when you might be notified: could be next week
or the week after that. Or, you might never hear from us at all."

One Thursday afternoon, Wayman's luck ran out.
He had just completed a form for a motor truck
manufacturing establishment, handed it in to the switchboard operator
and was headed happily out. "Just a minute, sir," the girl said.
"Please take a seat over there. Someone will see you about this."

Wayman's heart sank. He heard her dialling Personnel.
"There's a guy here willing to work full time
and he says he'll do anything," she said excitedly.
Around the corner strode a man in a suit. "Want a job, eh?" he said.
He initialled one corner of the application and left.
Then a man in a white coat appeared. "I'm Gerry," the newcomer said.
"This way." And he was gone through a doorway into the plant.

"We make seven trucks a day," Gerry shouted
standing sure-footedly amid a clanking, howling, bustling din.
"Over here is the cab shop, where you'll work. I'll be your foreman.
And here is the chassis assembly . . ." a speeding forklift narrowly missed them

". . . and this is where we make the parts."
"Wait a minute," Wayman protested, his voice barely audible
above the roar of hammers, drills, and the rivet guns. "I'm pretty green
at this sort of thing."

                 "Nothing to worry about," Gerry said.
"Can you start tomorrow? Monday? Okay,
you enter through this door. I'll meet you here."
They were standing near an office marked *First Aid*.
"We have to do a minor physical on you now," Gerry said.
"Just step inside. I'll see you Monday."

Wayman went shakily in through the First Aid office doors.
"I need your medical history," the attendant said
as Wayman explained who he was. "Stand over here.
Thank you. Now drop your pants."
Wayman did as he was told. "You seem sort of nervous to me,"
the aid man said, as he wrote down notes to himself.
"Me, I'm a bit of an amateur psychologist. There are 500 men
in this plant, and I know 'em all.
Got to, in my job. You shouldn't be nervous.
Remember when you apply for work you're really selling yourself.
Be bold. Where are you placed? Cab shop?
Nothing to worry about working there: monkey see, monkey do."

Then Wayman was pronounced fit, and the aid man escorted him
back through the roaring maze into the calm offices of Personnel.
There Wayman had to sign for time cards, employee number, health scheme

and only just managed to decline
company credit union, company insurance plan, and a company social club.
At last he was released, and found himself back on the street
clutching his new company parking lot sticker in a light rain.
Even in his slightly dazed condition,
a weekend away from actually starting work, Wayman could tell
he had just been hired.

"When I began this job, I was struck by the feeling that being isolated all day inside the huge barn of the truck plant was like being inside the vast hold of a ship. I had a kind of image of us putting out to sea, working away in the hold all day, and then returning each afternoon to the dock where we were let ashore . . ."

THE FACTORY HOUR

The sun up through a blue mist
draws its own tide: this is the factory hour.
As I drive east, I pass dozens like myself
waiting on the curb for buses, for company crummies,
for car pools; grey plastic lunch buckets,
safety boots, old clothes. All of us pulled
on the same factory tide.

                             The plant's parking lot
is the dock; the small van of the industrial caterers
has opened at the furthest gate through the fence: coffee, cigarettes,
sandwiches. Walking in through the asphalt yard
we enter the hull of the vessel.

The great hold is readying itself for the voyage. Steam
rises slowly from the acid cleaning tanks
near the small parts conveyor and spray booth.
We pass to the racks of cards; sudden clang of machine shears
but otherwise only the hum of voices, generators, compressors.
Click and thump of the cards at the clock. The slow movement
of those already changed into blue coveralls.

The hooter sounds, and we're cast off. First coughs
and the mutter of the forklift engines.
Then the first rivets shot home in the cab shop's metal line.
Air hoses everywhere connected, beginning to hiss, the whir
of the hood line's drills. The first bolts are tightened:
the ship underway on the water of time.

Howl of the routers: smell of fibreglass dust.
Noise of the suction vacuum, the cutter, the roar
of dollies trundled in for a finished hood. And the PA endlessly calling
for partsmen, for foremen, for chargehands:
Neil Watt to Receiving please, Neil Watt.
Jeff Adamanchuck to Sheet Metal.
Dave Giberson to Gear Shop . . . to Parts Desk . . . Sub-Assembly.

The hooters marking the half-hours, the breaks,
the ship plunging ahead. The PA sounding
Call 1 for the superintendent; Call 273; Call guardhouse; Call switchboard.
Lunch at sea: sprawled by the hoods in ordinary weather
or outside at the doors to the parts-yard if fine; whine of the fans
and the constant shuttling of the forklifts
show that the ship still steams. Then the hooter
returns us back to the hours of eyebolts,
grilles, wiring headlamps, hoodguides, shaping and
sanding smooth the air-cleaner cutouts. On and on
under the whir of the half-ton crane, rattle of the impact wrench,
grating of new hood shells as they are dragged onto a pallet.

To the last note of the hooter: the boat returned to its City.
a final lineup at the timeclock, and out through the doors
to the dockside parking lot. Late afternoon:
I drive into the tide of homebound traffic, headed west now
still moving into the sun.

70

"Only men work in this factory. The next poem is about the second stage of the line where fibreglass truck hoods are prepared for painting by having headlights, radiator grilles, etc., installed. The hood at this station is supported by a metal jig, which lifts the hood up high enough so one man can work inside or under the hood while another man works outside . . ."

THE JIG

Andy and Bill are at work at the second station
of the fibreglass hood line: Andy is under the hood shell
that is fitted over the metal jig. The hood sits
as it will on the finished truck
but now with a man under it, not a motor.
Bill begins to drill holes in the shell
for lights and reflectors. Andy comes out for a moment and the two
hoist the radiator grille into place. Andy goes back inside.

Andy has worked here ten years. Before this he was a railroad switchman
in Canada and California. He did a term in the U.S. Army,
applied for citizenship but returned to Vancouver.
When he started here, the job began with a piece of sheet metal. Now
it's all assembly of parts formed elsewhere:
"like a giant Meccano set," he says. Six years ago
he got home from work to find his wife had left for Oregon
with his children. He went after them and discovered
his wife was in a mental institution, his children
placed in foster homes. He collected his kids and came back
but a social worker followed him north and convinced him
the children would be better off where they were.
Support money was wanted, though, and recently an Oregon county
has begun suing Andy. "Why should I send money?" Andy says.
"The kids won't get any of it. My ex-wife and the guy she lives with
are both real drunks, winos, and that's where the money will go.
When she left me, it took four years to pay off the debts

she'd run up. Now they want me to pay more.
It's like I'm being punished for something I didn't do."

Outside the hood Bill smokes his pipe
as he pushes through the bolts to hold the grille.
He is twenty-one, worked here five months.
He laughs cheerfully as Andy complains a bolt is too short.
"Angry Andy, Angry Andy," Bill says. No reply. Bill has been married
three months, and a first child is on the way.
Each coffee break and at lunch he is on the parts-desk phone to his wife.
"She's home alone in the apartment," he explains.
"It's only fair." Bill met his wife
a few months before they were married.
"I'd known her a long time earlier, though," he says.
"It's strange: I'd completely forgotten her. I'd been up
at Ashcroft for a year or two on a commune. When I got back
I met a friend who said she was in town again.
I couldn't remember who she was at first, but when I did
I said, 'Let's drive over and see her.' We did
and she had just broken up with her boyfriend or something.
Anyway, we went out together a few times and I knew
she was the one I wanted to marry."

He fondles his wrenches, screwdrivers, and ratchet, re-settling them
in his toolbox with his pipe and tobacco pouch.

"I knew she was the right one for me," Bill says seriously.
"I can't imagine ever going with anyone else."

Now he chuckles as Andy mutters something glum
out of the semi-darkness under the hood. Inside, Andy lifts
the impact wrench to the nuts he has fitted
as Bill outside puts his wrench to the head of each bolt.
For an instant as the nuts are tightened
the two are joined across fibreglass and metal.
What are they building this afternoon in their lives?
A 623 hood, marked for turnlights,
fender braces, grilledenser, and a large air-cleaner cutout.

"Once each year the routine work of the plant is stopped for a two- or three-day event known as inventory, which sends everyone everywhere peering into bins and climbing over racks noting down how much of everything is still left after a year's production.

"Naturally, I was assigned to work outside. And, naturally, outside it poured rain . . ."

INVENTORY

Standing in the parts yard all day
in the heavy rain, rows of us
dressed in the cheap plastic dayglo hooded jackets
and waterproof pants the company bought for
inventory, gloves soaked through
in the first twenty minutes of
reaching into the heavy wooden ring pallets
to pull out the dripping metal parts.

Larry and I began with steps: the metal beaded with rain,
water pouring out of the bent-in corners as
each step was lifted out to be counted: all the different ways
a man's foot can climb up onto a truck
with him not thinking for a second how
that step got there, formed from an expanded bar
of aluminum, or galvanized iron, given a certain number
in the factory where it was made, shipped to this place,
provided with another number that is stamped on it somewhere
and now, perhaps months or more than a year before anyone stands on it
the step gets taken out in the midst of a steady October downpour,
is counted and tossed back in
with somebody noting down its number and how many there are,
his sleeve dripping onto a damp card as he tries to write.

And the forklifts pass splashing through the maze of
pallets brought out into the aisles between the parts-racks

where wet figures in the bright orange plastic suits
bend over the contents—unidentified tubes, pipes, bars and castings
jumbled beside them—and others have climbed up ladders
and over the frames of the racks
to curse and keep counting in the endless rain.

Larry and I did mouldings next, and the following day
brackets, from massive metal plates to aluminum ones
so thin and tiny their assigned number
has to be hammered into wired-on metal tags
now lying nearly submerged in the puddles on their shelf.

Truck parts, in the rain. The water
soaking in at last through the stitching of my boots
as though I had hiked for hours down the mud
of a rainforest trail. In the woods: moss and ferns and the huge cedars.
Here, plastic and wet metal, asphalt and the trundling forklifts.
And nothing will come of this rain
but money

and part of a truck.

"It costs money to go to work: clothes, tools (on this job we had to provide many of our own hand tools), you eat more, you need more entertainment. The next poem considers how so much of our money is accounted for as soon as we've earned it . . ."

WHAT IT'S DONE FOR

Two hours each morning—from the first hooter
until first break—are worked for the government.
For this an alarm clock sounds in an empty room,
I get up in the dark rain and go out
to the door into the plant again and begin
under the lights with our dust and drills.
"If that much goes in taxes," Bob says,
"I'm just going to goof around until coffee."
But he doesn't.

       And I work
an entire week out of four for the landlord
so I can sit here in the evenings
looking out over the City rain.
Five mornings to climb out of sleep
into the steadily moving clock and five afternoons
returning to wash off the day, make supper
and eat it, clean the dishes for breakfast
and make the next day's lunch and pack it
and wait. All for the landlord: a week of the steady tiredness
that nibbles vaguely at my time off like
faint small sounds of someone's television
heard continually through the walls, ceiling or floor
as though the body could hear its own breathing.
And the landlord sits
two flights down and waits for my week
to be handed him once a month as a slip of paper.

And I work for a food store, for a new strap
on my wristwatch, and oftener than I'd like
for the manufacturers and distributors of auto parts.

Of the minutes I spend at work
one after another until they make up an hour and more
hours until break by break my lunchbox is emptied
and one whole day is completed
—how little of this is brought home for me to spend
in the time before I have to go to bed
to get up to go back to work once more.

"People have various ways of dealing with the routine of the job. One partsman, Neil Watt, used to go around pretending the material we were working with had a life of its own. If he saw me drilling holes in the fibreglass hood shell, for example, he would make a big deal about reporting me to the SPCF: the Society for the Prevention of Cruelty to Fibreglass.

"This idea of Neil's got me off on a fantasy of my own, but to acknowledge my debt I call this Neil Watt's Poem . . .*"*

NEIL WATT'S POEM

At first metal does not know what it is.

It has lived so long in the rock
it believes it is rock.
It thinks as a rock thinks: ponderous,
weighty, taking a thousand years to reach
the most elementary of hypotheses, then hundreds more years
to decide what to consider next.

But in an instant the metal is pulled into the light.
Still dizzy with the astounding speed
with which it is suddenly introduced to the open air
it is processed through a concentrator
before it can begin to think how to respond.
Not until it is hurtling along on a conveyor belt
is it able to inquire of those around it
what is happening?
We are ore, is the answer it gets.

A long journey, in the comfortable dark. Then the confusing
noise and flame of the smelter, where the ore
feels nothing itself, but knows it is changing
like a man whose tooth is drilled under a powerful anaesthetic.
Weeks later, the metal emerges as a box full of bolts.
What are we? it asks. *Three-quarter-inch bolts.*

The metal feels proud about this. And that is a feeling
it knows it has learned since it was a stone

which in turn makes it feel a little awed.
But it cannot help admiring its precise hexagonal head
the perfectly machined grooves of its stem.
Fine-threaded, someone says, reading the side of the box.
The bolt glows, certain now it is destined for some amazing purpose.

Then it comes out of its box and is pushed
first into a collar, *a washer,* and then
through a hole in a thin metal bar.
Another washer is slipped on, and something
is threaded along the bolt, something else
that is made of metal, *a nut,* which is whirled in tight
with great force. The head of the bolt
is pressed against the bar of metal it passes through.
After a minute, it knows the nut around itself
holds a bar of metal on the other side.

Nothing more happens. The bolt sits astonished
grasping its metal bars. It is a week before it learns
in conversation with some others

it is part of a truck.

"Mostly, however, the routines of the working life are inescapable . . ."

ROUTINES

After a while the body doesn't want to work.
When the alarm clock rings in the morning
the body refuses to get up. "You go to work if you're so keen,"
it says. "Me, I'm going back to sleep."
I have to nudge it in the ribs to get it out of bed.
If I had my way I'd just leave you here, I tell it
as it stands blinking. *But I need you to carry your end of the load.*
I take the body into the bathroom
intending to start the day as usual with a healthy dump.
But the body refuses to perform.
Come on, come on, I say between my teeth.
Produce, damn you. It's getting late.
"Listen, this is all your idea," the body says.
"If you want some turds so badly you provide 'em.
I'd just as soon be back in bed."
I give up, flush, wash, and go make breakfast.
Pretty soon I'm at work. All goes smoothly enough
until the first break. I open my lunchpail
and start to munch on some cookies and milk.
"Cut that out," the body says, burping loudly.
"It's only a couple of hours since breakfast.
And two hours from this will be lunch, and two hours after that
will be the afternoon break. I'm not a machine
you can force-feed every two hours.
And it was the same yesterday, too . . ."
I hurriedly stuff an apple in its mouth to shut it up.

By four o'clock the body is tired
and even more surly. It will hardly speak to me
as I drive home. I bathe it, let it lounge around.
After supper it regains some of its good spirits.
But as soon as I get ready for bed it starts to make trouble.
Look, I tell it, I've explained this over and over.
I know it's only ten o'clock but we have to be up in eight hours.
If you don't get enough rest, you'll be dragging around all day
tomorrow again, cranky and irritable.
"I don't care," the body says. "It's too early.
When do I get to have any fun? If you want to sleep
go right ahead. I'm going to lie here wide awake
until I feel good and ready to pass out."

It is hours before I manage to convince it to fall asleep.
And only a few hours after that the alarm clock sounds again.
"Must be for you," the body murmurs. "You answer it."
The body rolls over. Furious, and without saying a word,
I grab one of its feet and begin to yank it toward the edge of the bed.

"To make our time off work more enjoyable, most of us acquire a wide range of gadgets from cars to cameras. These technological wonders often seem to me to get mixed up with the very fabric of our lives: our relationships with others, and with ourselves.

"One of my friends at work was telling me about an incident which struck me as a good example of this . . ."

ANDY'S TAPES

I was over at the redhead's place, my new girlfriend's
last night, and borrowed some old records she has
to tape them. But when I got back to my apartment
I started to listen to the tapes I was going to erase
and use over. These are the ones
I made with Mae, right after I got the recorder.
When we were going down the Oregon Coast together
each spot we'd stop at one of us would say something about the scene
so we could remember it. And once I put the microphone
under the bed: she was sure mad when she found out later.

I was three years with her. I listened to the tapes
until one-thirty, then I erased them.
There are some pictures of her I'm going to get rid of, too.

"Another break from routine in the working life is the strike, if you happen to be working in an organized place. Whatever may be said about the decline of the union ideal into big-business bargaining agents, whether American- or Canadian-controlled, there is still something awesome to me in the power those of us have who build the world every day. This is a poem about that . . ."

THE OLD POWER

The old power is still here: pulling into work one morning
to find the access road to the company parking lot
jammed with men and vehicles, more cars
piling up behind, spilling out onto the main street
and down adjacent lanes, everybody arriving
from different directions to stand together
at the gate of the almost-empty lot
(just a few foremen's cars and the night shift of painters)
where five men from the company's sales and service division
on strike for more than a month now
stand with their picket signs.

Early morning dark, and a cold rain.
Five men with sheets of cardboard looped around their necks
changing feet to keep warm, drinking coffee
from the small white cups somebody brought them:
five men in a line, occasionally talking to someone else
but mostly just standing at the very edge of company property
and then a little space
and then all four hundred of us, mixed in
with our lunchpails and boots and the cars that brought us here.

Like an old myth that suddenly works: a marvellous event in a forest
that happens to you personally so that again
you can believe in what you once had clung to
and then abandoned: five sheepish men

in the rain at the end of a road
hold back our hundreds. And this is something
both of us make: they carrying the symbol out in front of us
and we agreeing. So whatever happens here
is ours.

After half an hour in the drizzle, the sky getting lighter,
not a supervisor or foreman in sight,
some of us wander off to the Lougheed Hotel for coffee.
Then, I drive home. And all the while the five men stand there
like pillars of the old power, an idea made flesh,
an idea that works. So that today, Thursday,
no one has to build a single truck

and we can take all the rest of this day in the rain for ourselves.

"The next poem is about a difficulty I have always had with violence. Being a practising coward, I have never understood so many people's apparent willingness to beat each other up . . ."

VIOLENCE

The cars leap out of the plant parking lot
lay rubber, fishtail, and disappear.

Bill says: "The scar? When I was up in Ashcroft
I was coming out of the pub one day and a guy I'd never seen
smacked me in the face with a piece of wood.
Broke these teeth and split me open along here: nose, lips, chin.
I got stitched up, and the next day
had a buddy drive me around town looking for the guy.
I saw him, told my buddy to stop
and leaped out holding a tire iron behind my back.

"The guy recognized me. He comes up and says:
'I'm sure sorry about yesterday. I thought you were somebody else.'
I said to him: 'You have three seconds to start running.'
He turned to get away, and I let him have it across the back of the head.
Cold-cocked him right there in the street.
Then I kicked the shit out of him, broke a couple of his ribs
and me and my buddy got out of there fast."

And Magnowski, the giant partsman, on his wedding night:
"They put shaving cream, lather, all over my car.
I stopped in at a garage to wash it off
and as I was using the hose the attendant comes out
and just stands there, making all these dumb comments
like: 'I guess you're really gonna screw her tonight, boy.'
I couldn't believe it. He was big, but

I'm a head taller than him. I was going to deck him
but it was our wedding night. Debbie was right there in the car
and I'm wearing a tuxedo and everything.
So I just said: 'Do you have a hose with some *pressure*
in it, asshole?' He got kind of choked up at that.
He could see I was really mad, just holding myself in.

"But I didn't want to ruin it for Debbie on our wedding.
I think I'm going back this Saturday and see if the guy is still on."

And Don Grayson, another partsman, limping around
with a broken foot he got kicking someone
in a fight in the Duff beer parlor.
He and his friends took exception to some remarks
that were made about the woman who brings the food.
And me always careful not to get in a fight.
Chris and Ernie, Bucket and Phil at lunch one day
talking about a brawl, and me saying:
"It takes two to fight. If you don't want to
you can always walk away." And Ernie really horrified
at this: "Oh no, Tom, no, no.
There are times when you have to fight, you just have to."
And me maintaining that you don't
and everybody looking disgusted at my idea.

How is it I have clung all my life to my life
as though to the one thing I never wanted to lose?

Bob changes the subject. We begin to talk about car accidents.

94

"A lot of the talk at work is about each other's personal situation: relationships and families. A number of the people I met are members of an organization called the Burnaby Single Parents Association—which pretty well sums up the state of many families. I have a poem about this called The Death of the Family *. . ."*

THE DEATH OF THE FAMILY

"You married, Tom?"
No, but the girl I'm going with is.
To someone else. Ha-ha. You see . . .

But they aren't listening.

"Tom, I was going with a woman
for two years. A few weeks ago she asked if I was going to marry her.
I told her I might someday, but, hell,
I was married all those years
and once I got my divorce I'm not in any hurry to do it again.
I didn't say I wouldn't *ever* marry her.
I just said I didn't want to right now.

"She says to me: 'Dave, if you don't want to marry me
I'm wasting my time.' And that was it.
I tried to call her up a couple of times
but she said if I didn't hang up she would hang up on me.
Bang. Just like that she stopped seeing me.
I think she's crazy. I know she hasn't been seeing anyone else
but she'd rather sit at home and see nobody
than go around with me anymore if I won't marry her.
I just want someone to visit after work, to go dancing with.
And there's something else: she once told me
if we got married, she would come first.
She meant, before my kids. I have two, and there's her three

but she says she has to come first.
There's no way: my kids come first with me.
Who else is there to look after them?"

       And young Bob
over from Cab Build for the morning, to help out when we're behind:

"My Mom walked out on us twice.
After the first time, when she wanted to return
my Dad he took her back and it was okay for a while.
Then she left again. And you should see the guy she went off with:
a drunk and everything."

     Then through his mouth
the voice of his father: "We treated her like a queen
but it wasn't enough for her."

All over the plant, through the long hours.
Up to Test to replace a grille's side shell, I hear Jim Pope's steady voice:
"When my first wife left me, I phoned in to take the day off.
I had the locks changed by ten o'clock, and was down to the bank
to make sure she didn't get a cent.
Then I went over to check about the car registration.
You have to move fast when it happens . . ."

Someone in the small group of coveralls
is receiving advice.

"But no matter what gets talked about at work, the routine goes on. A friend of mine, who is one of those people who is always getting into trouble, used to hum a blues refrain that I liked. Eventually I stole it and used it as the first verse in the following song. To ease my conscience, I call the whole song his . . ."

BOB KINE'S SONG

I got those
Monday morning blues.
I got those
Monday morning blues.
Right down to the bottom of my steel-toed shoes.

Spent the whole night looking at the alarm clock,
had it set for six-fifteen.
Spent the whole night looking at the alarm clock.
I had it set for six-fifteen.
Woke up at seven-thirty: O Lord, I'm late for work again.

Jumped in my car and drove
as fast as it would go.
Jumped in my car and drove it just as fast as it would go.
Ran out of gas on the freeway; cold rain falling, mixed with snow.

Found a phone booth and called the foreman:
told him what my troubles were this time.
Yes, I phoned in to tell the foreman what my troubles were this time.
He said: "Bob, you were late three times last week, missed eleven days
in the past two months and left early eight times since January . . ."
—I should have saved my dime.

And when I got to the factory
he had me back on the rivet crew.
Yes, when I finally got to the factory he put me back on the rivet crew.
Bucking those rivets all day with Schultz: don't know if I can make it through.

So I went upstairs to the washroom
to snort some coke and take my ease.
Went upstairs to the washroom to snort some coke and take my ease.
Just when I have it unwrapped on the paper, then of course I had to sneeze.

And I forgot my lunch money:
eating a candy-bar one more time.
Yes, I forgot my lunch money: eating a candy-bar one more time.
If I don't get out of this factory, people, I'm about to go out of my mind.

I got those
Monday morning blues.
I got those Monday morning blues.
Lordy, Lordy, right down to the bottom of my
steel-
      toed
           shoes.

"Monday is bad, but the weekend is great. I have a little poem here in appreciation of Saturday especially . . ."

SATURDAY

Somebody's car won't start. O-
kay, get dressed fast and into
the street, bright cloudy morning,
fresh wind and the sea lying
grey down in the inlet. Dig
my jumper cables out from
under the back seat, drive half
the block to his car, hook up
and his engine catches, and
we're off to the garage with
me following to be sure.
Wait by the Saturday side-
walk, drive him back. *Thanks,* and I'm
in for a wash, breakfast, and
a long easy chapter in
something. Then it's after ten.
Whoops. Everything piled in the
sink, and it's downtown tripping
around. Look at some records,
books, a store with marvellous
knives and forks, some new shirts. What
do I buy? A new pair of
work socks, a pen refill, then
back over the Bridge 'cause it's
nearly four. Into the crowd

at the meat market, then on
to the jumble of carts in
the Safeway, up and down the
aisles, with my list for the week's
collection of bottles and
tins and small plastic bags full
of various vegetables
and some cookies and gum for
the job, also bread for my
sandwiches and a big square
container of milk for my
thermos. Then back to the place
to unpack and phone the girl
for a movie or maybe
just dropping down to see Doug.
Then stick a potato in
and goof while it's baking, then
salad and boil broccoli,
meantime frying up a nice
fillet that was on special.
Pile all in the sink again
after, and I'm gone.

"We are considered unskilled labor in the plant where I worked. But near the end of my stay there I added up all the various tasks I was supposed to be able to do. I thought back to school, and what an examination might look like if someone was being tested on this knowledge.

"Incidentally, in the following, the term 'unitglass' that is mentioned is the company tradename for the type of fibreglass used . . ."

UNSKILLED LABOR

Good morning. On the table in front of you
you will find question sheets and answer booklets.
You have four hours to complete this examination.
When you have finished, please hand your answer booklets
in to me, with the question sheets inside.
The exam is divided into six sections: grilles,
unitglass hoods, fenders, folding hoods,
assembly operations and general plant knowledge.
Are there any questions? Very well, you may begin now.

I Grilles.   For three marks each
describe and differentiate between the following grille parts.
Be sure to explain which specific unitglass hood each grille part is used with.

a. K137-72 grille screen   h. 106 and 106R side shells
b. K137-143 ″   ″   i. 1522 bottom shell
c. K122-11 grilledenser   j. 522   ″   ″
d. K212-100 top shell   k. K167-119 moulding bar
e. K212-110 ″ ″   l. K167-120   ″   ″
f. 79 and 79R side shells   m. K167-175-6   ″   ″
g. 138 and 138R ″   ″   n. K167-226-2   ″   ″

II Unitglass Hoods.   For three marks each
describe and differentiate between the following unitglass hoods.

a. K146-748   d. K146-651
b. K146-747   e. K146-630
c. K146-623

III Fenders.   For fifteen marks
    describe and differentiate between any four types
    of metal and unitglass fenders in use at this time.
    Provide the Kenworth numbers for each type you discuss.

IV Folding Hoods. For three marks each
    describe and differentiate between the following folding hood parts.

    a. K146-793 hood   e. 2641 hood side
    b. K146-795   "   f. 585 and 585R hood sides
    c. K146-736   "   g. 584 and 584R   "   "
    d. 2640 hood side

V Assembly Operations.
    1. (5 marks)   What is the Bill of Materials (B.M.)?
        What can we find on it?
    2. (15 marks)   Describe the complete assembly
        of any specific grille you choose. Be as thorough as you can.
        (DON'T just say: "the top shell is then bolted on"
        but list, if you can, the various specific dimensions
        of the nuts, bolts, washers, etc. used in attaching the top shell.)
    3. (15 marks)   Describe the complete assembly
        at the first Hood line station
        of any specific unitglass hood you choose. Be as thorough as you can.
    3a. For 2 BONUS marks: differentiate between a 2215 electrical harness
        and a 2549 harness.
    4. (17 marks)   Describe the complete assembly on the jig

of any specific unitglass hood you choose. Be as thorough as you can.
(HINT: Don't forget the 117 and 118 hood guides!)

4a. For 2 BONUS marks: differentiate between 177, 204 and 204R hinges.

5. (4 marks)   Describe the complete assembly
of any usual sub-assembly operation in the hood department.
(HINT: This could be make-up of any hood stop cable, eyebolts, etc.)

6. (15 marks)   Describe the complete assembly of any specific fender
—unitglass or metal—you choose. Be as thorough as you can.

6a. For 2 BONUS marks: differentiate between a proper hood dolly
and a proper fender dolly. Where are these to be found in the plant?

7. (15 marks)   Describe the complete assembly
of any specific folding hood used on the line (Assembly II).
Begin with the hood blank, and be as thorough as you can.
For the purposes of this question, hood sides
—whether attached or not—are to be considered part of the hood
whose assembly you are to describe.

8. (15 marks)   Describe the complete fitting
of any specific folding hood and sides used in Bay Build (Rigid Frame).
Be as thorough as you can.

VI General Plant Knowledge.   For one mark each:

    a.   Who is the plant superintendent? Where can you find him?
    b.   Who is the general foreman (for assembly)? Where can you find him?
    c.   Who is the cab shop foreman? Where can you find him?
    d.   Who is the cab shop chargehand? Where can you find him?
    e.   Who is the hood department partsman? Where can you find him?
        (NOTE: No sarcastic remarks here, please!)
    f.   Who is the folding hood partsman? Where can you find him?
    g.   BONUS mark: Who is the cab build shop steward? Where
        can you find him?

108   *"The next poem was written looking back on this job. It's called* How I Made It Through . . .*"*

HOW I MADE IT THROUGH

The heft of the small compressed air drillmotor
under the fluorescent lights
The slow ease of its drillbit passing into fibreglass

Fine ridges of the threads of small bolts
lifted out of the full trays of parts
Thin, cool washers of stainless steel are slipped on
and the bolt, held by its hexagonal head
is set in through a hole in the grille side, into the hood

Or, assembling a grille, peeling back the layer of paper
unwrapping the polythene inside that
to bare at last the clear body of the freshly-chromed
metal top-shell, a perfect mirror
Pulling the last of its covering away, to leave it new and
naked: beautiful

Hands put into blunt gloves
to make the trim and air-cleaner cuts in the fibreglass
with router and saw
The rasp of sandpaper and files
straightening and rounding the hood's new edges
The lift of the hood onto a dolly, straining
to tilt its weight on its hinges, and fit
the dolly's strut supports

And against all this, carrying me through:

the feel of my finger tips passing
on her smooth, firm, taut skin
warm in the glow of a yellow lamp, in the whispering darkness

"And the last poem . . . is self-explanatory . . ."

THE KENWORTH FAREWELL

Everyone wore eyeglasses for safety.
To Wayman at first the factory had the look
of a studious crew of graduate students
dressed by mistake in torn and baggy coveralls
who had wandered in through the high aisles of stacked parts
to stand aimlessly amid the machines and assembly stations.

And the boys in Cab Build
were hooting: *Whoop. Whoop.*

Settling in, getting to know the place, Wayman discovered
both box-end and open-end wrenches, fine- and coarse-threaded nuts.
Also the forklifts, which never failed to release
a warm fart of propane when Wayman passed behind them.
And Wayman meanwhile got real intimate with his wristwatch:
staring at each minute in every hour
until somehow it turned into a morning, and even an entire day.

And the boys in Cab Build
were hooting: *Whoop. Whoop.*

Wayman returned home each late afternoon to the rebirth of a bath:
the grand feel of fresh clothes against his skin.
Picking the dirt out of his nose, he understood
not only was he in the factory, the factory was in him, too.

So he learned all the Kenworth slogans:
"It's only a truck", and "It's only a Kenworth",

and "At sixty miles an hour, who is going to know the difference?"
Also: "There's a right way, a wrong way,
and a Kenworth way." And Wayman mastered
the Great Kenworth Fault Game: "It isn't *my* fault."
Even if an error took only a minute to fix
like forgetting to drill safety light holes, for example,
everyone argued happily for hours
all the cosmic questions and implications
of each other's ultimate innocence and guilt.

Wayman learned the faces, and what each meant.
Working with young Bill was a rain of washers
he and Larry endlessly tossed back and forth.
Wayman discussed women with so many, only to later discover
they were just out of high school and still living at home.
And there was the day Gerry the foreman complained about the quota:
"I have seven hoods to get out today, but what do I have
to do it with? A hunky (meaning Daniluk)
a hippie (meaning Wayman)
and a God damn sky pilot . . ." (meaning Wayne
who before Wayman left finally cornered him
and gave him one pamphlet on the Four Spiritual Laws
and another called—Wayne said: "Don't worry about the title"—
Jesus and the Intellectual.)

And the boys in Cab Build

were hooting: *Whoop. Whoop.*

Wayman might have stayed forever.
But his first clue was a Monday morning
when it seemed the weekend had never occurred.
The second clue was Paul Palmer telling him
(Palmer the mainstay of the Pipe Shop's
Hose Amputation Division):
"I've worked at this bench a year, but it feels as though
I might have been here one day, or always."
And so often the great gleaming $50,000 trucks
wouldn't start at the end of the Final Line
and had to be towed out into the yard—which broke Wayman's heart.
Also there was a moment when Wayman found himself
in his own car rolling down the highway near Bellingham:
heading north again on a Sunday, but driving just the same
on that beautiful concrete freeway which he knows also drifts
south in a dream towards California.

So Wayman at the end picked up his toolbox
shook hands with the foreman
and walked out another time through the Kenworth Keyhole:
that man-sized door set into a truck-sized door
on which someone has thoughtfully painted "Door".
Wayman passed out of the world of tires and fibreglass dust,
timeclocks, and the long sessions upstairs in the can.

And as the boys in Cab Build
howled their last farewell: Wayman
was on his way once more.

THE CHILEAN ELEGIES

"In the fall of 1973 the human race suffered a setback when the elected government of Salvador Allende in Chile was overthrown by the Army. A social experiment—to see if a peaceful transition to a form of democratic socialism is possible—was halted by the bullets of another general's revolt. The new regime quickly imposed the customary brutalities of a Latin-American military dictatorship.

"These events came at a time when it seemed in my own life there was no organized opposition to the bosses in my country that a person still in possession of his faculties would wish to work in. I wrote five elegies to the slaughter in Chile which intend to touch also on the conditions of our own life. The five elegies are followed by a coda, and finally a seventh poem . . ."

THE CHILEAN ELEGIES: 1. SALVADOR ALLENDE

The wood comes from a living tree
brought down, ripsawed into rough boards
and nailed together into parts-boxes and forklift pallets.

Dust has settled onto the battered wood:
a heavy dust, from metal that is drilled and pounded,
from fibreglass that is cut and shaped, and from the weariness
of the hands and legs that have done this day after day.
Eyes have looked at this dust every lunch break
and at our ten minutes mid-morning and mid-afternoon.
Dust from overtime, and carried in
on the wind from this factory's City.

Allende is dead. I have not followed the newspaper
for three years: the news is what happens to me.
Now he is dead another layer of dust,
black grains, has sifted in among the stacks of truck parts.
The dust makes a faint sound as it settles
like a man who sighs, far away. I believe Allende's dust
is falling into every factory in the world.

It says that whatever you might want
there is no reason to vote. Men are alive who are killers
and not a word or a vote anywhere can stop them.
If you love your life there will never be change.
This is one more thing the poor know
in every factory. And now Allende is with us
in the dust on the concrete floor.

"Among those who died in the coup in Chile was Pablo Neruda, one of the greatest poets of our century and I think of all world literature. Neruda won the Nobel Prize for Literature in 1971 and was a complex figure. He has poems which describe exactly what it is like for a child's foot to be imprisoned in a shoe . . . he has that much sense of freedom. At the same time, he was an orthodox Communist— the Communist Party's candidate for President in the last Chilean election—and took no stand counter to Russia's treatment of its dissenting writers.

"In his poems Neruda speaks of the poor and working people of Chile and the Americas, and about what it is like to be a man alive on the planet in our time. The earth, the ocean, the air and the creatures that live and die there flow through his work. His poems are as likely to speak of geology and geography as history or biography, but everywhere their main concern is humanity . . ."

THE CHILEAN ELEGIES: 2. NEFTALI REYES

"Pablo Neruda" was the pen name adopted by the
young student-poet Neftali Reyes.

This does not mourn Pablo Neruda.
I speak here the death of Neftali Reyes.

Neruda goes on in the ocean of words
that is his life forever. Certainly he was stopped
before he said everything, but in that
how is he different from anyone else?

But Neftali Reyes is dead.
He died of a cancer called The Modern Army:
a cancer present in every country. In Chile, in Canada, an Army
day after day is patiently training to kill.

That is all it is for. It cannot so much as make its own rifles
or run a railroad for very long. And it has no one to shoot
but its brothers: neither an invasion of Eskimos
nor penguins threatens, and against the wars
of the U.S. or Russia what could it ever attempt?

Yet in each state, the President or Governor
keeps the uniform of the High Command in his closet.
Sometimes he wears it only on special occasions
but often enough it is pulled on each day.

As it was on the final day of Neftali Reyes.
He was one of a thousand *chilenos*
struck down that day by the Army. And like each one

suddenly pulled into the sea of death
his mouth filled with so much salty blood
that for once and for the last time it was blood, human blood
that poured over his lips and chin instead of a song.

Neftali Reyes is dead. But the great wave that broke over him
was scarcely a ripple to the sea Neruda
moving on the Neruda earth. Despite the deaths of so many,
the death of Neftali Reyes, as with the lives of so many
the life of Neftali Reyes,

Neruda sails on with his cargo of poems, with his freight
of coffee, bathtubs, typewriters, carpenters
grasses, electricity and the poor: goes calmly on
through space, carrying the living and the dead
carrying the dead body of Neftali Reyes
carrying the dead body of Neftali Reyes

on the great Earth: pablo neruda.

THE CHILEAN ELEGIES: 3. PABLO NERUDA

124

It was as if a cruel winter
descended on the coast of Chile
locking the water and soil
into a vise of snow and the cold.
Somewhere in the white emptiness
near what had been Valparaiso
an immense glacier moving down from the mountains
calved an iceberg with the sound
first of a pistol shot
and then a colossal groaning and thundering
that echoed and echoed all over the frozen world.

Falling away from the seaward edge of the glacier
the iceberg, in its second of birth
shot huge plumes of water high in the noisy air:
the calling of seabirds rising for a thousand miles.
The ice bobbed once, settled comfortably into its marine existence
and began travelling steadily. Against every current
every belief that in books is considered natural law
the iceberg floated north. Crossing the Pacific equator
it shrank some, but grew again as it passed the mists of
Oregon, the heavy rain of the Washington coast.

One afternoon it appeared at the end of my street.
When I returned from work, a small crowd
stood at the doors of my apartment building
talking about it. Like an advertising campaign

it was not unexpected: we have read so much
by certain navigators
about these matters, that when at last the iceberg floated
here in the harbor off Kitsilano Point
how could I be surprised? And it has come up Yew Street
climbed the stairs to my room
and knocked on the door. It has entered my blood
and started up the hot streams of my arteries
melting toward my heart.

Growing on top of the ice
is one tiny rose, imperfectly formed, a rose
that can only grow in the dirt
but nonetheless is alive on the ice.
When the iceberg enters my heart
I think only the rose will be left.

And it is the rose that will stay
in my heart forever.

And where it says *they shot so many factory workers*
does it mean Larry Tetlock
who began at this factory three months before me
after the usual adventures working for Sears
hanging drapes: trying to install new white ones
with a spiral screwdriver someone had loaded with oil
and having his van catch on fire
from a faulty battery one day while making deliveries?

Is this who they mean? Larry, at 20
with a brand new Vega to drive and working
to pay for it, intending to look for another job
if we strike, fed up with the din of this one?

Or is it Ernie they killed? Ernie, who jumped
from the Hungarian Army in '56, learned English
and used to work at General Paint?
Thirty-six and divorced, he was back to Hungary twice
and realizing he would work at the same place here or there
elected to stay with racetracks, stereos, and all the movies he can see?
"I'm always happy," Ernie says, one day
when everybody is angry at him for being so dense.
"I never get depressed. No." Why do they want
to put an end to his jazz collection, his nights
in the Ritz Hotel beer parlor?

But these aren't the men who have died.

These will be back at work Monday, and Tuesday, and also Friday
firing Huck bolts and lifting their end of the fender
until they quit and get another job
or until I quit and sit in a room writing lines
until I too get another job. Not Vancouver, but in Santiago
in those rainy graveyards surrounded by old houses
partitioned into suites, family areas, and rented rooms
fresh earth is dug, and a sound of crying
a shriek, and a heavy silence goes on
for entire avenues, so many people put into the ground
like fill for some seedy construction project
involving the mayor, his uncle the contractor, and the pay-off
of a number of zoning officials and building inspectors.

Except that it's death. What do they think a man understands
who works in these places, a man only the newspapers
and certain theoreticians of the Left consider "a factory worker"
a man who believes himself simply to be his own name
—Larry Tetlock, for instance? Why does an order go out for his death?

What if the first thing he knows about bullets
except for a friend who has offered to take him hunting
is the bullet inside his own head that the Army intends
to let him keep forever? What do they think he sees
that they want to sever the optic nerve
so what the eyes take in will never get to the brain

and from there to his hands?

Why cause this disruption in production:
no end of trouble and re-scheduling for
foremen and chargehands, not to mention whole families?

Why should they kill Larry Tetlock?

THE CHILEAN ELEGIES: 5. THE INTERIOR

The smell of potatoes just taken out of the earth.
The problem every carpenter faces, where the wood
nearly fits. The man who secretly wants to leave his wife
and only his fantasies keep his sexual life alive.

These things no government can alter or solve.

The lineup in the small bank branch on East Twenty-ninth
after work on Friday: old boots and the shapeless trousers,
short windbreakers whose sleeves end in hands that clutch
the paper that means life. Other lines
that have worried their way into the faces above the eyes.

These mean an ache for money that lasts an entire lifetime
from busfare each morning through to the tiny pension.
These mean it is luck that rules: the wisps of lotteries, horses,
or entering the pool each payday for the best poker hand
that can be gathered from the company's number on your cheque.

Also, applying when they're hiring: no government
has been able to touch that.

The small towns of the Interior. The railroad towns deep in the forest.
What has the government to do with them?
The struggles of the young teacher
who has arrived to work in the school
mainly of Indians. All the arguing
with the principal, and with the old librarian,

the enthusiasm carried into the desperate classroom.
And the Indians themselves. Their new hall
they built themselves at Lytton, which had to be boarded up
after a month because of the damage. The summer camp
they built twenty miles away in the mountains
where a young boy drowned the second week it was open.
It too is abandoned again to the silence.
Potato chips and Coke the staple food of so many.
And television, television, television . . .

On the Thompson River, or in Parral
the government is not the government of the Indians,
not of the young teacher, not of the townspeople,
not of the lover, the carpenter, the man who digs potatoes in his yard.

But where a government takes the remotest of steps
to return home to the ground, and when even this small gesture
is embargoed, denounced, plotted against
and at last some incredibly expensive aviation gasoline
is pumped into certain jet fighters donated by another government
existing thousands of miles away
there is a loss that goes deeper than the blood,
deeper than the bodies put into the ground,
that descends to the roots of the mountains
and travels that far down in the crust of the planet
along the continental chains

until all over the world another sorrow is confirmed
in the lives of the poor. Once again
we are made less. There are men and women
who in the cells of the fibres of their being
do not believe the Indians are dying fast enough
do not believe the poor are dying fast enough
do not believe that sickness and hunger,
automobile crashes, industrial disasters
and the daily suicides of alcohol and despair
are ridding the earth of us with sufficient speed.
So they call for the only institution
maintained at the highest possible level of efficiency:
the men with guns and capbadges, willing or conscripted,
whole armies and the tireless police. These are the men
who have made of this planet throughout my life
a vast geography of blood.

*So many shot for subversion in Temuco. So many arrested
for drunkenness in Lytton.*

And there is not a government in the world that wants to abolish the factory.

CODA: A CHILEAN INCIDENT

Two soldiers are lifting a dead man
out of the rubble of a factory.
They have lashed together a tripod and are winching the body
up through a hole of shattered concrete, splintered wood.
The factory was Chilean, bombed by the Chilean Air Force.
The men alive are Chileans, as was the dead man.
It seems to me there is no such thing as a country:
there are men and women, and there are also men and women.
The lines into the wreckage are taut now:
the dead man is almost up to the surface.

And after they have brought him this far
they go on lifting him. The people who work at the Civic Morgue
say they were cautioned not to reveal how many bodies arrived
and what happened to them, under penalty of arrest themselves.
But they say that after dark, load after load of bodies
were transferred into Army helicopters
which lifted off, lights blinking, into the noisy night
headed steadily west. Once out at sea, beyond Valparaiso
a door was opened in the side of the aircraft
and the cargo dumped into the air.

That instant over the Pacific
is as high as the Army wants to carry the dead man.
As they gave him his death, so they give up his body
to the long fall through dark wind, and the water.
A dead man descends through the blackness, through the white spray

of the sea's surface, and deep into the colder, darker ocean
wrapped in an Army shroud. He falls
further than any winch made by anyone in any factory
ever can lift him out now.

"The seventh and last poem of this series refers in part to an event in Neruda's life when he was once forced to flee from the Chilean dictator González Videla. Aided by the poor of his country, as he tells in his poems, Neruda escaped over the Andes and fled to France.

"In my poem, after the poet's death the body of his poetry moves secretly through the Chile of the dictator Augusto Pinochet and continues on across the earth . . ."

THE RETURN

The poet comes back.
After the agony in the great stadiums
suddenly converted into prisons:
the torture of the young woman
in the corridors under the bleachers,
the rape and beating of the journalist's wife
while he is watching, the daily executions,
the electrode making contact again and again
on the body of the student strapped face-up on the table:
its black point darting in like the tongue of a snake
now searing the scrotum with terrible pain, now the tip
of the penis, now the inside of the lower lip,
the nipples, the tongue, now the eye is forced open
and the electrode brought down toward the pupil . . .

After his body is stilled, the poet returns.
He knows that no one jailed the former Ministers of Health
when the new government began for the first time
to distribute milk to the poor.
But the hands of a woman who worked in that program
now never stop shaking.
No one wished to interrogate the local executives
of a foreign mining company
about the long years of sorrow and sweat wrung out of Chile.
But there is a miner who lay on the concrete and bled inside

from the kicks of the police, until he died.
And no one sent for a squad of torturers from America
to investigate those Americans found living in Santiago
after the election. But a certain unit of the Brazilian military
instructed in the American school in Panama, and in their own country
flew in to begin processing their countrymen
discovered after the coup to have previously fled into Chile.

And there is a woman who heard so much screaming
she can no longer utter a sound.
There is a body dropped from an Air Force truck
into the street of a slum, that only on close examination
can be seen to have been a woman.

But the poet comes back.

His breath, his voice, his book
once again begin journeying.
His country goes down again
into the horrible night of its continent
but the poet continues to move.
Everywhere he comes to the poor like a man in trouble
and is taken in or not depending on their nature.
Those who receive him risk everything
just as though they hid again the living fugitive
but, as before, when he leaves he departs as their friend.

Those of the poor who are fearful, and turn him away
go on being poor, being frightened, still waiting
for the miraculous knock on the door that they know
will one day arrive to show them a better life.

The poet goes on. His words
are specks of light gleaming out of the darkness.
Death surrounds us all, but his words
go on speaking out of the blackness.
Hunger still sits in the stomach
like an egg soured into a chemical burning in the guts.
The muzzle of a gun is still pressed against the head of a man
who is shot before he can say a single syllable.
The voice of the poet is powerless to stop this.
The man who is beaten, his front teeth
snapped off under the sticks of the police
—he, too, loved the sound of the fresh salt wind
pouring in continuously over the waves of the sea beach . . .

But to everyone left numb
in the silence between these cries of agony and despair
the poet's voice goes on talking, calmly, persistently.
Also through the long drudgery of a lifetime
it keeps offering to those who have lost them
the words that mean a gift of the earth.

The poet says: "They burned my house in Madrid,

the house of flowers, geraniums, and a green horse.
They pulled down my house at Isla Negra,
brought down its great ceiling beams carved with the names
of dead companions, lowered my flag: sea-blue, with a fish on it
held in and let free by two chains.
And when I saw the house of poetry was destroyed again
I knew that poetry now would be most needed elsewhere.

"So I began travelling. When I was alive
I took my place in the struggle. Now I am dead
my voice still speaks, ringing like a vast silence
which is really a mouth, filled up one by one
by those who take up my cry, which is their cry,
sounding our words together, drowning out torture
and the police, louder, drowning out hunger and fear,
louder, drowning out sickness and want, louder and louder,
speaking our life on this planet as loud as we can
until at last we drown out death."

THE KISS AND THE CRY

"Not to end on such a note, I have here three poems about a fairly common experience: the ending of one relationship between a man and a woman and the beginning of another. The first poem, called Untangling, looks at the discovery that familiarity is sometimes the main factor giving life to a relationship . . ."

UNTANGLING

A man and a woman living together a long time
are an organization, a small makeshift company
operating from a storefront, a tiny corporation
that creaks and groans and has its own peculiar filing system
that nevertheless can usually be made to produce
what those running it want to find again.

Working for it is deeply unsatisfying:
no matter how hard you try you can't seem to do a good job.
On assembly, you're always parts short,
the specifications have been changed,
the one part of the job you figured you had cold
the leadhand has just told you he doesn't like how you do it.

Personalities get accommodated
with the automatic gestures of two men carrying a board
they have already lifted each day for a month.
Or with all the effort spent in bringing a pet cat
into somebody's room: food has to be stored away, a catbox
put out, certain windows must be kept shut. Then it's a year
since you last really looked at her face.

None of this considers events: someone crying
at the breakfast table, while somebody else
goes calmly on eating. On shift
you can't wait for coffee and for quitting time
but walking out to the parking lot you feel a little incomplete,

off work until tomorrow. Or maybe leaving for good:
that means a part of your life
marked off and left back there like yesterday's timecard,
like talking about the details of your last job,
like starting again to look for
another necessary tangle.

"Starting to search for a new relationship, I have found, always puts me back into an adolescent world of dates, nervousness, etc. It is bad enough to go through an adolescence at 15 or 20, but at 30 it is especially humiliating and silly. Still, it seems necessary, so what can you do . . . ?"

WAYMAN IN CIRCULATION

After more than two years, Wayman and his girl call it quits.
Wayman reaches for the phone again, delighted, but as he is dialling
an old scar floats to the surface of his psyche like a bubble in hot water:
what will the woman he is about to call think of his squeaky voice?

And in the days that follow, each of Wayman's old anxieties
reappear: how do his armpits smell?
Every terror he was sure he had safely outgrown
he now discovers was off taking classes growing bigger
and meaner and cleverer: did he brush his teeth?
What *is* he supposed to do at her door saying goodnight?

Wayman finds he has stumbled out of all the ease
of a customary relationship
into a new nervous world where he wants to make a good impression.
But he has to pick his nose, even if just for a second.
And if he lets this fart out slowly, perhaps she won't notice it's him?

Two years older, his emotional life
once more transformed into a puddle of apprehension and despair
Wayman is back in circulation.
Despite his frightening interpersonal history, however,
his endless betrayal by his body

Wayman has a date for Saturday night.

"And the last poem intends to deal with the changes I have noticed in myself and my world. It is called The Kiss and the Cry . . ."

THE KISS AND THE CRY

When we first kissed, that November night
I heard the faint noise of crying.

I drew away my lips. In the cold air
someone was sobbing.

She pulled me back to her. We kissed again, mouths opening,
tongues beginning their first discoveries
of where the warm blood goes, pulsing, inside our flesh.

But the crying grew louder. Through my ears
I recognized the tears of the girl I had just broken up with
after two years. And without opening my eyes
I heard her joined by the hoarse masculine agony
that must be the husband of the girl I clung to now
—arms around the bulky fur and cloth of our coats—
the husband she had left six months ago.

Kisses and kisses. But the cold night around us
grew an avalanche of crying: the tears of her parents, and mine
for what we had done and what we intended. Tears added on
by those friends of ours who were bitter and lonely this evening
and the crying of others we didn't know who were likewise alone.
Tears of the City's married:
how none of their lives were like this moment,
tears of those worn out today at their work,
tears of the crippled, retarded, tears of the mad,

the strange, broken tears of the hungry, the sick,
and the effortless, hopeless, continual tears of the poor.

All this surrounded us, where we clutched each other in the night:
a howl and clamor filling the empty street
and the chill air. And I could pick out
the sound of myself crying: painful, uncontrollable gasps
of my chest and breath, spasms driven by some horrible loss
I had not yet discovered . . .

In the front seat of my car, where we embraced like adolescents
hands moving desperately over each other's bodies under our heavy winter clothing
though both of us nearly thirty,
I addressed the sound of so much misery:

If my sorrow added to yours could help, I said
I would give up joy.
I swear that, if I could, I would go right now to live in a different world:
some planet without this constant unhappiness.
But I no longer believe my pain
will help another human being.

And when I had said this, there was not a sound in the car
or under the street lights, except her breathing and mine.
I was very calm, very certain.
I think at that instant another person was born.

Born in Ontario in 1945, Tom Wayman has travelled widely in Canada and the U.S.A., working at jobs ranging from construction to college teaching. *For and Against the Moon* (1974) won the Canadian Authors' Association Medal for poetry. He has recently been appointed Writer-in-Residence at the University of Windsor.